I0753751

Windows Into War

(a mother's lament)

Windows Into War

(a mother's lament)

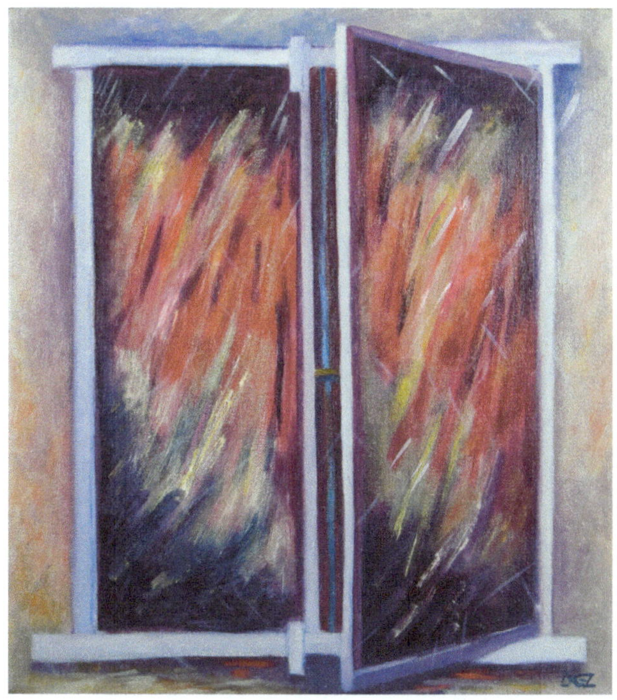

Poems and Paintings

by Deborah Gross-Zuchman

ABINGDON SQUARE PUBLISHING

New York

Windows Into War
published by Abingdon Square Publishing
463 West Street, Suite G122
New York, NY 10014 USA
www.abingdonsquarepublishing.com

Book design: Abingdon Square Publishing
Photographs of artwork by Gabriel Sim Laramie

ISBN 978-0-9823480-7-9
Library of Congress Control Number: 2010913499

Printed in the United States of America

This work is dedicated to my son Alex
and to mothers everywhere living in times of war

and to Philip Zuchman for his friendship,
guidance and love throughout our lives together.

Preface

Through paintings and poems, Windows Into War embodies my feelings as an artist, mother and American.

I have used the metaphors of windows and our flag to portray the losses, suffering and unraveling of the American democratic ideal.

The series is a cycle – beginning and ending with tulips. The theme of windows introduces the perspective views inside (fearful) and outside (hopeful). After taking the viewer through still life, landscape, abstraction and figure, explosive colors of fear, chaos, desolation and despair become softer and approach hope.

The succinctness of the poems is an integral part of the visual image leaving thoughts to be gained and little to be misunderstood.

The creative force is a powerful weapon that encourages life and beauty in overcoming death and destruction.

Deborah Gross-Zuchman
October, 2010

Still Life With Tulips

The flowers in my Spanish vase
Give us order; but we are not calm.
It is not about the tulips; but rather,
How they sit in a simple clay pot
In front of a window
With darkness creeping in.

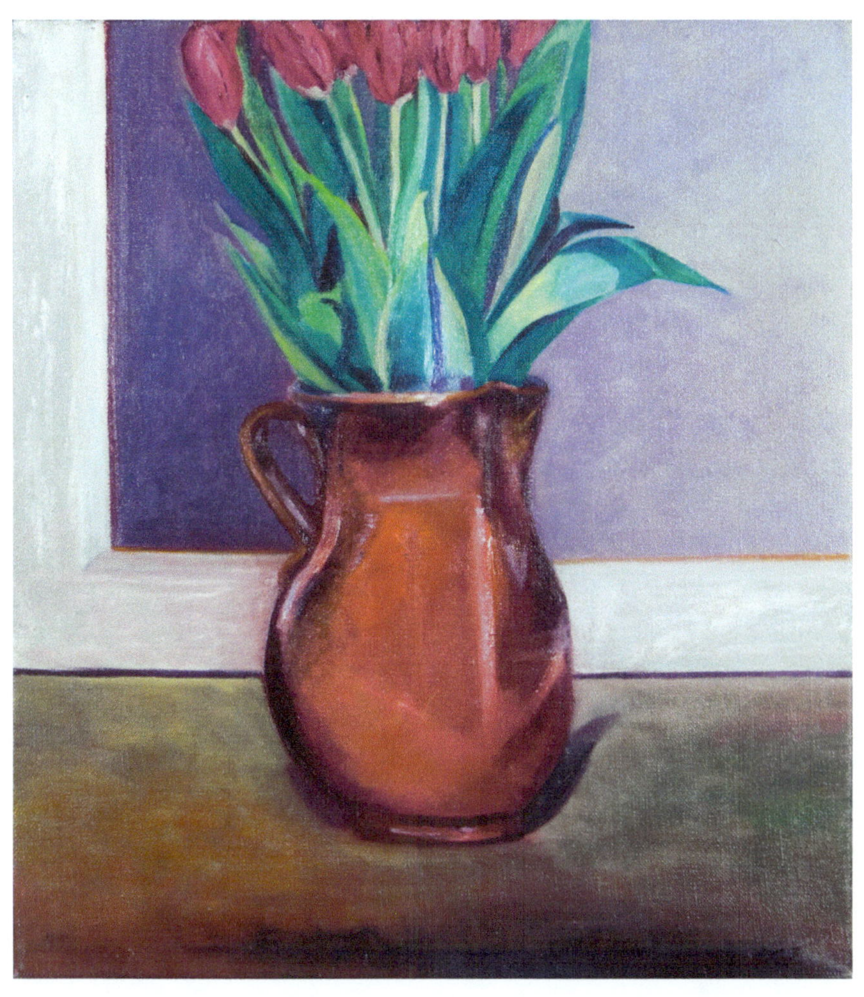

War

I am looking out my window
And I see the trees are marching
The grass is screaming
And the roaring fire will
Not let the sky be blue.
Soon the glass will break.

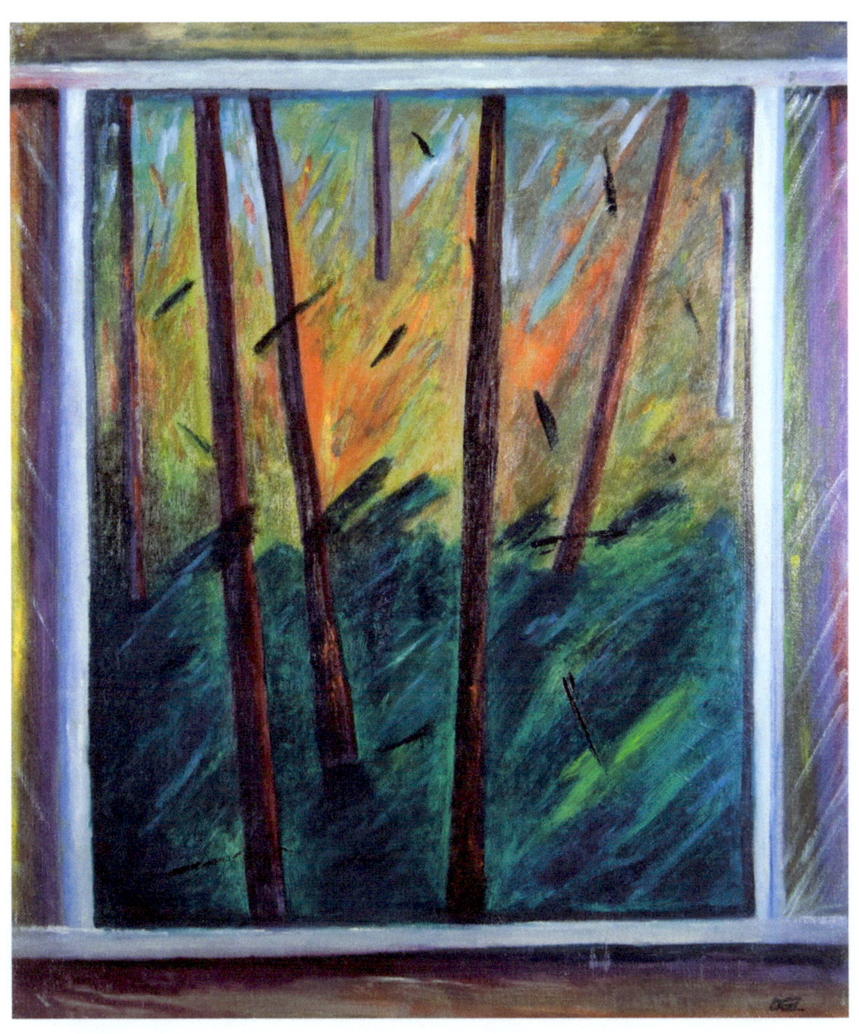

Opened Window

The opened window sees the chaos,
The fire and destruction.
Are we safe inside or
Is death coming because our eyes are closed?

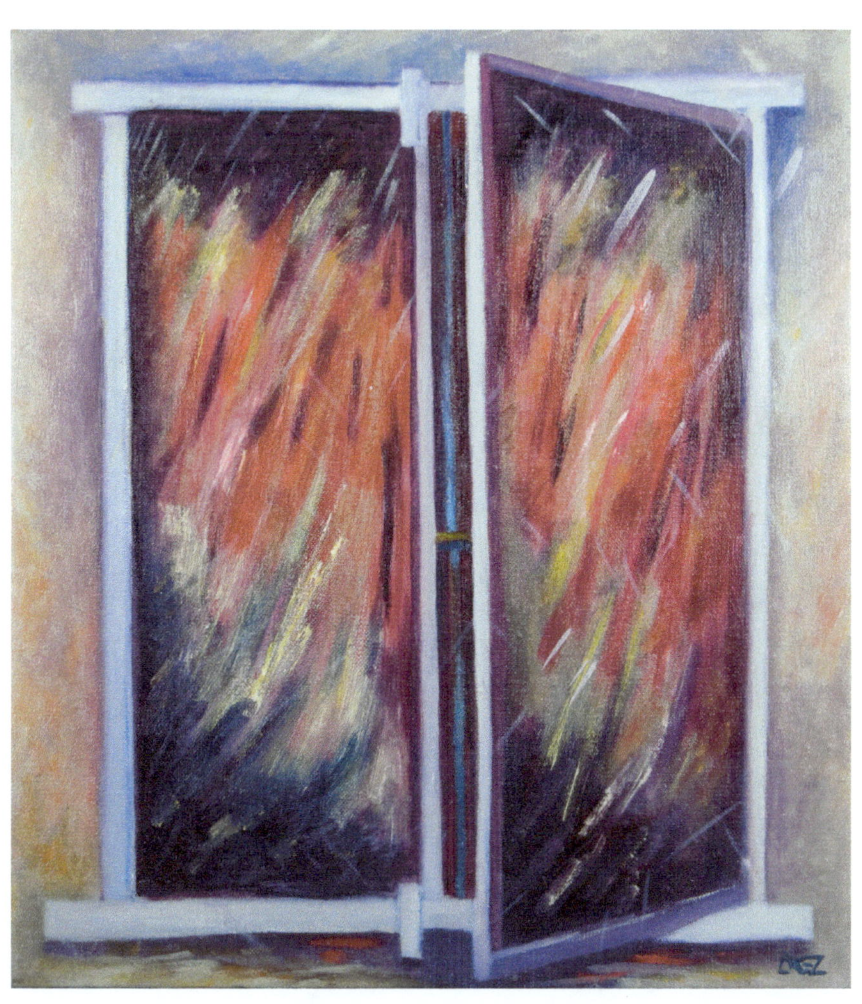

The Unempowered

It is safe inside and peaceful
But I look out and see the difference.

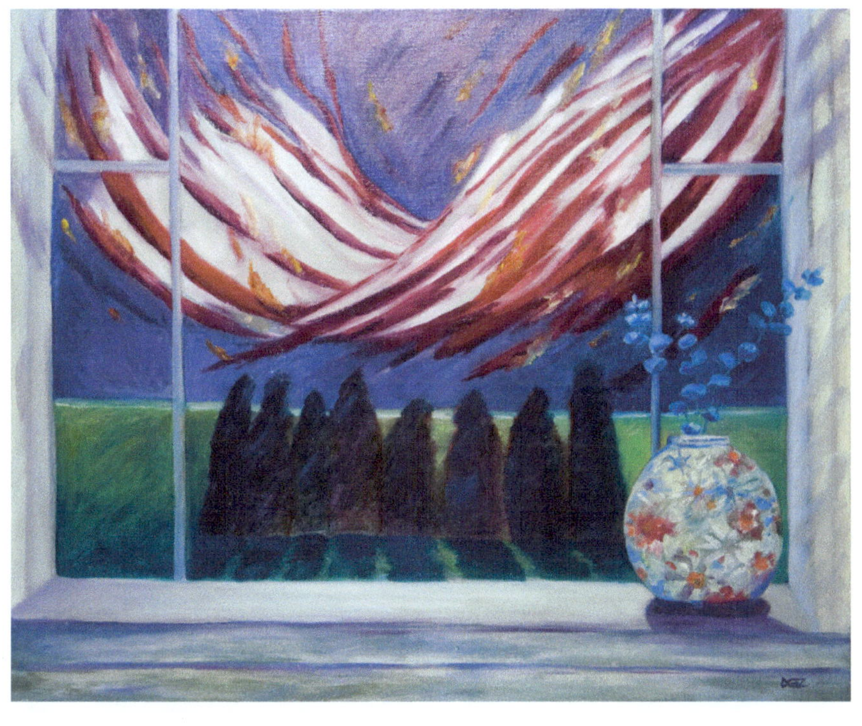

Fire

The land is burning
The sea is roaring
Where can one hide
When the earth is so angry?

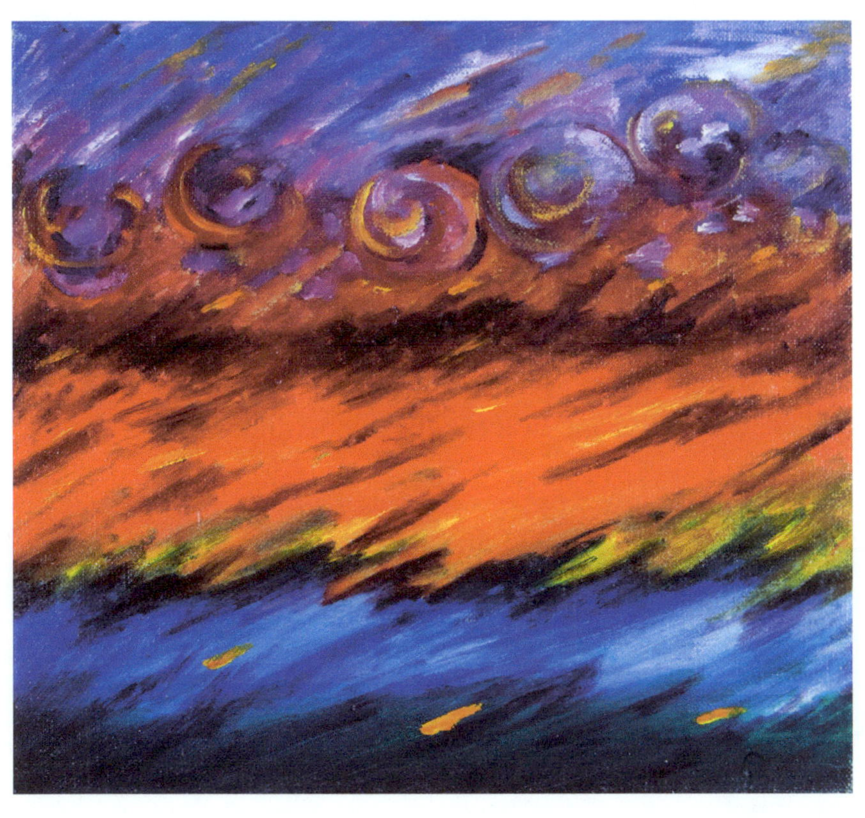

Unraveling

Who has shot my flag
And made it come undone?
I lifted up the window shade
And saw the stars falling
And the smoke was coming in my window.

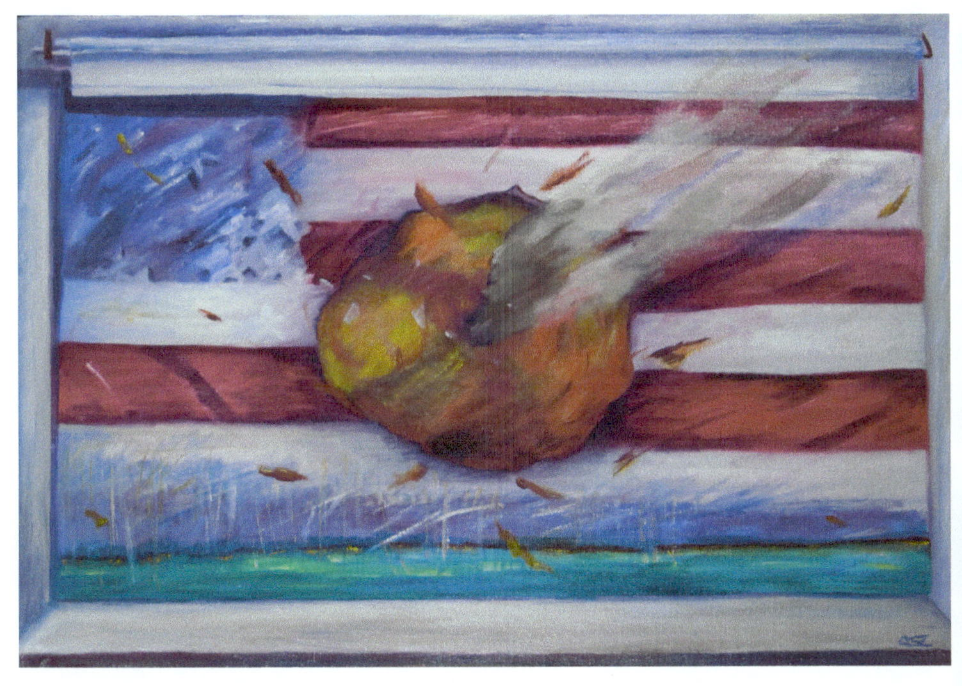

Shrouded Figure

I stand shrouded
Hoping to be protected
Covering my despair
Hiding my anger
That our American flag is burning.

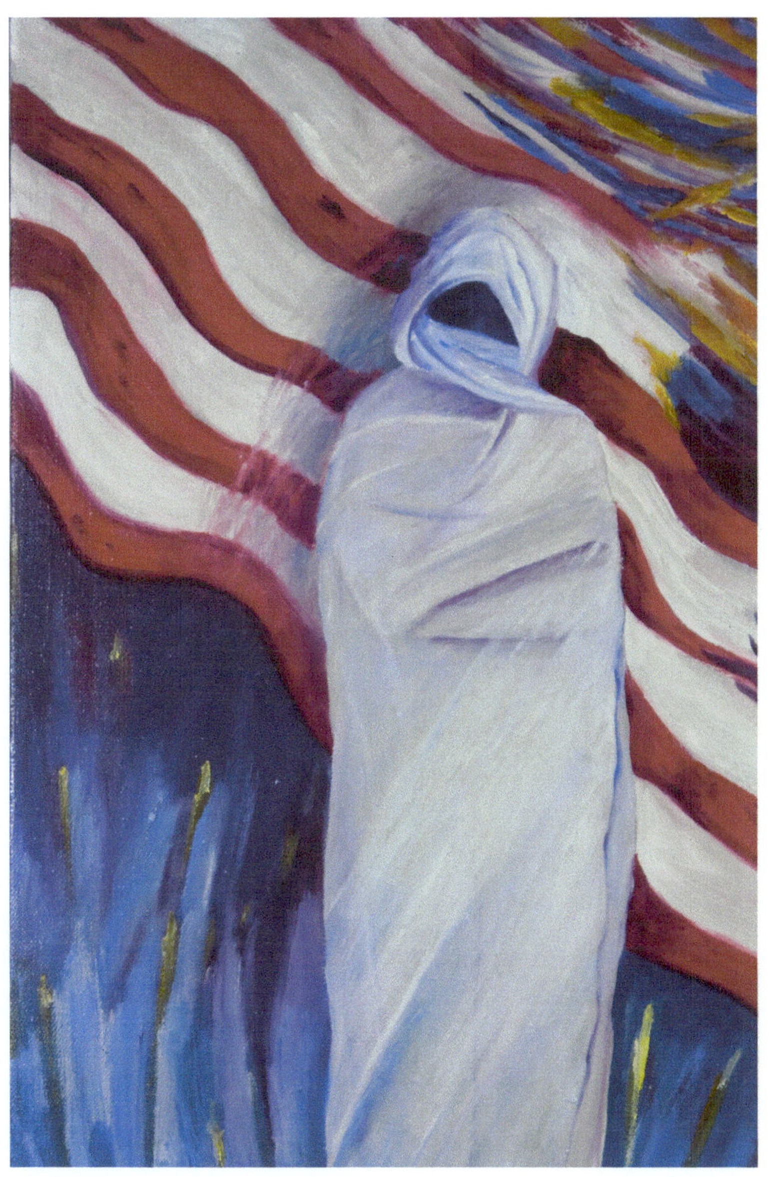

American Gothic Shaken

When we are talking war
The flag is put in front.
The posts of our fence,
Meant to protect us,
Are uprooted and fly away
The house is shaken, her stability broken.

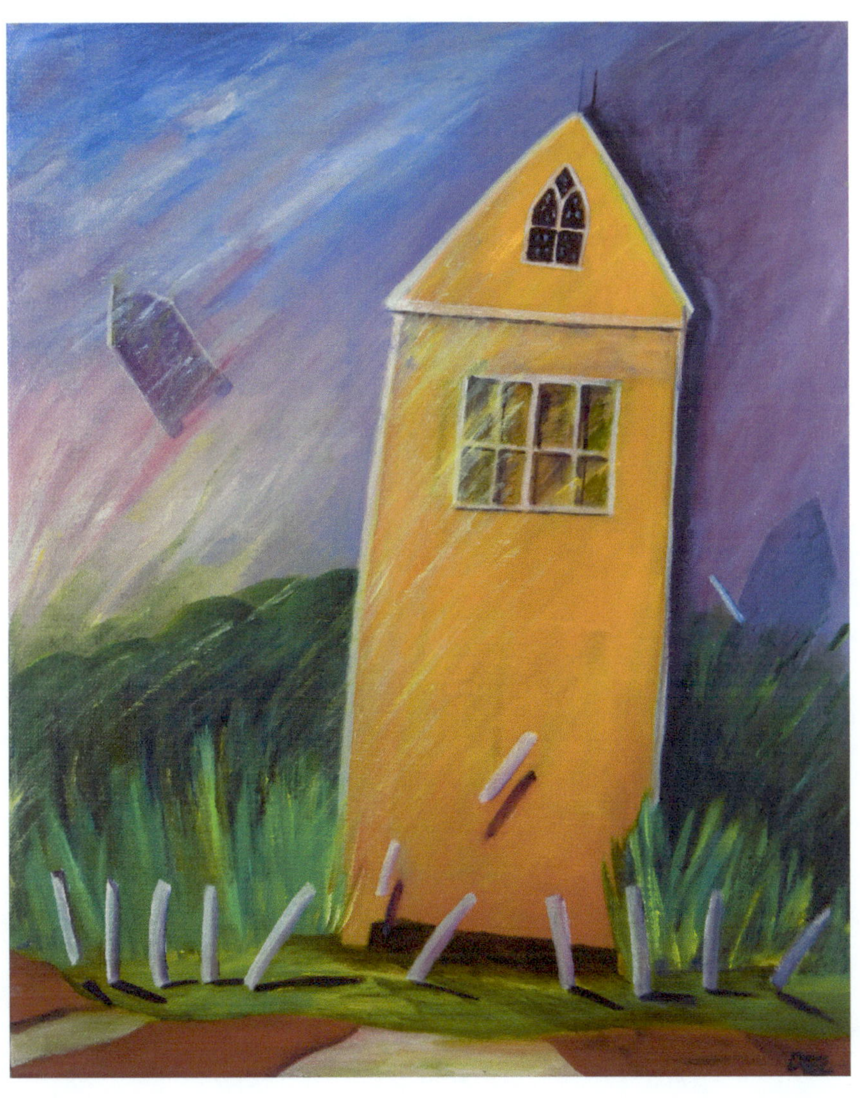

Gated Community

The flag is flying high
But its threads are torn.
The places we think safe
Are an illusion – or delusion
In time of war.

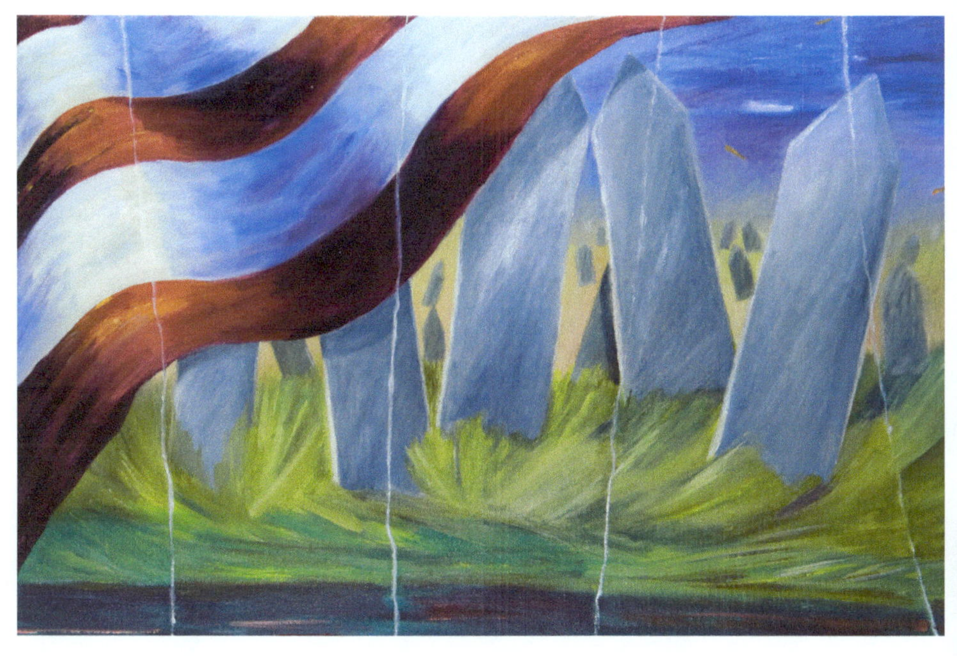

Peace March

They have all come
With their signs
Cloaked in their robes
Marching through the city, hoping
To gather those who wait in shadow, unsure.
Their flag holds them together
Ties them, bonds them – for
Who could love their country more
Than those who call for peace?

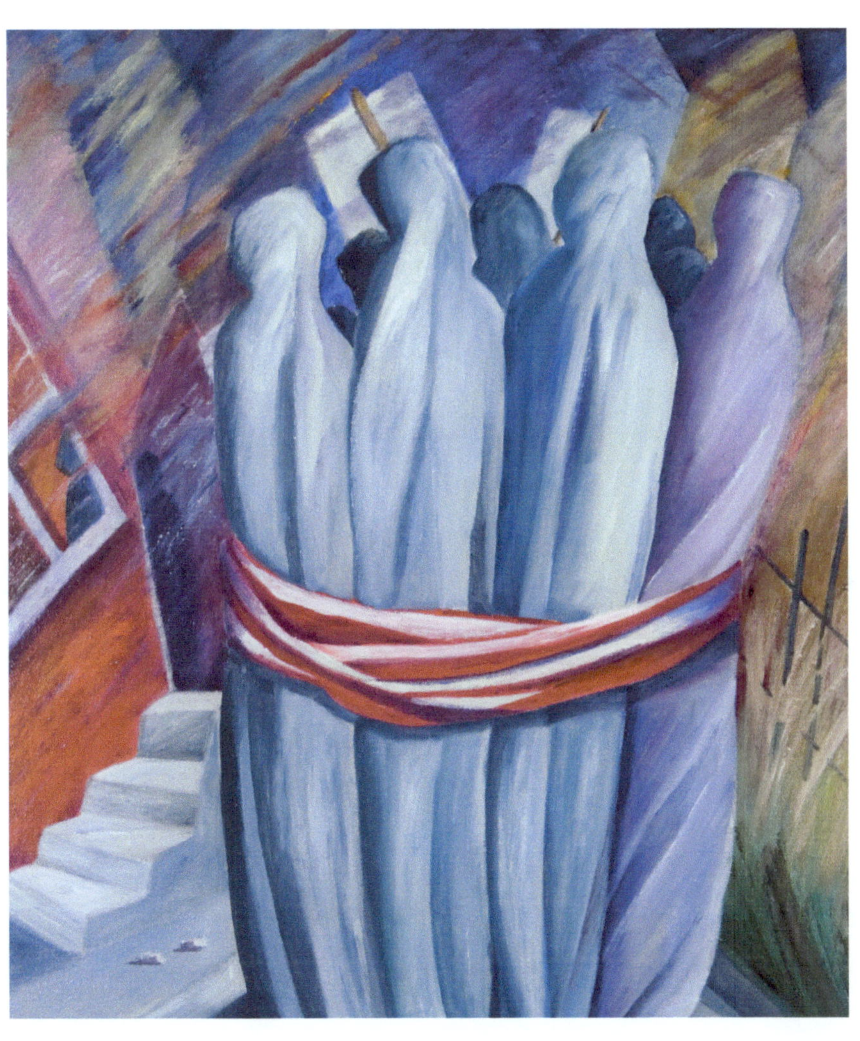

Fire On The Horizon

The flag is cresting with the waves
And the fire has lit the sky.
But what time of day is it?
Is the darkness being pushed away
Or will it blanket us to sleep?

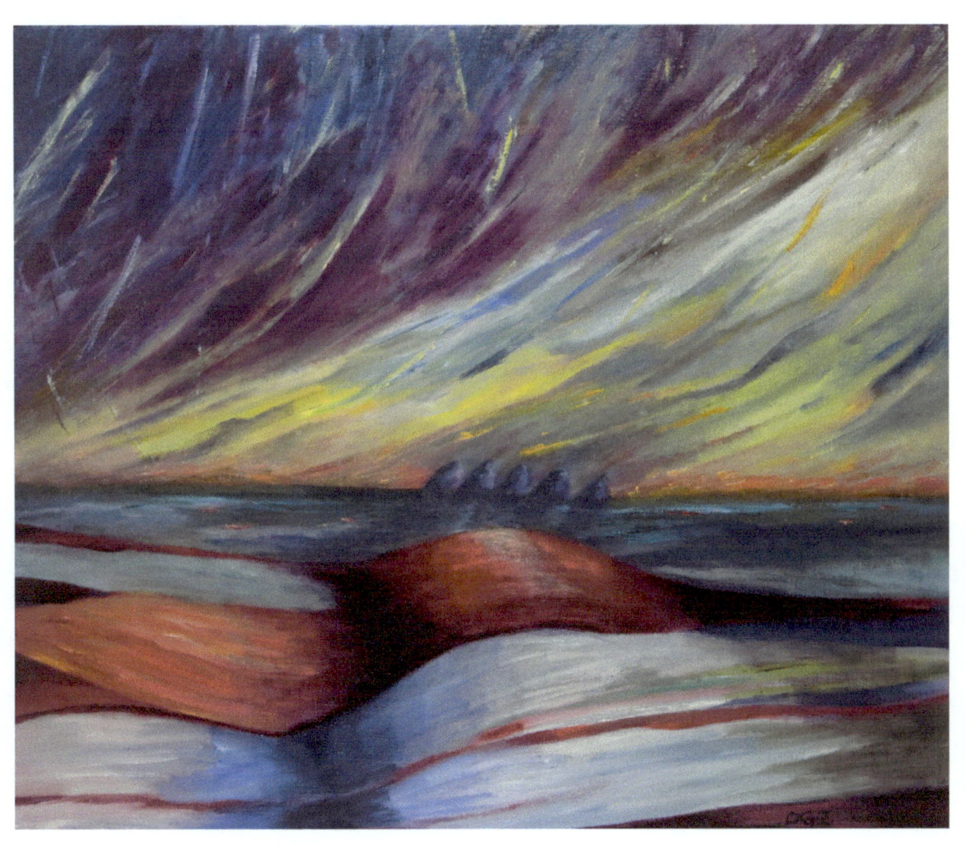

Desolation

I thought to call it hope
When I saw the rainbow fill the sky.
It came after the storm
And all was quiet.
But it was too quiet
And it had not rained.

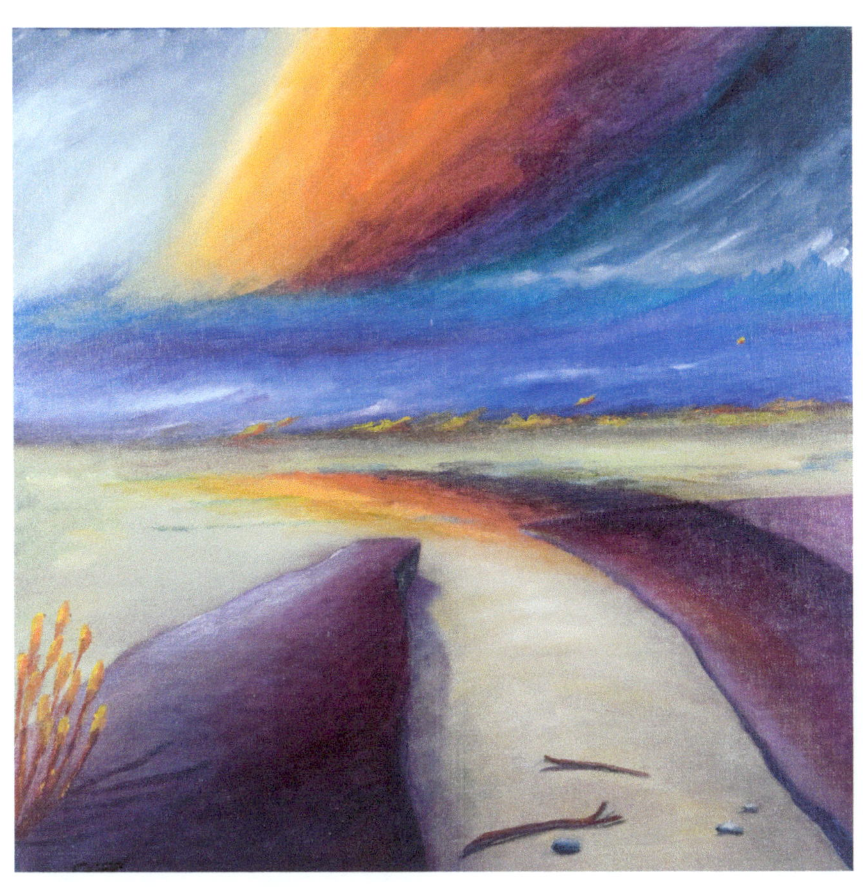

My Pieta

A mother holds her son
And asks why have you done this.
She is searching for an answer
When no answer can be found.
The son says, Mom, don't worry
But all mothers do.

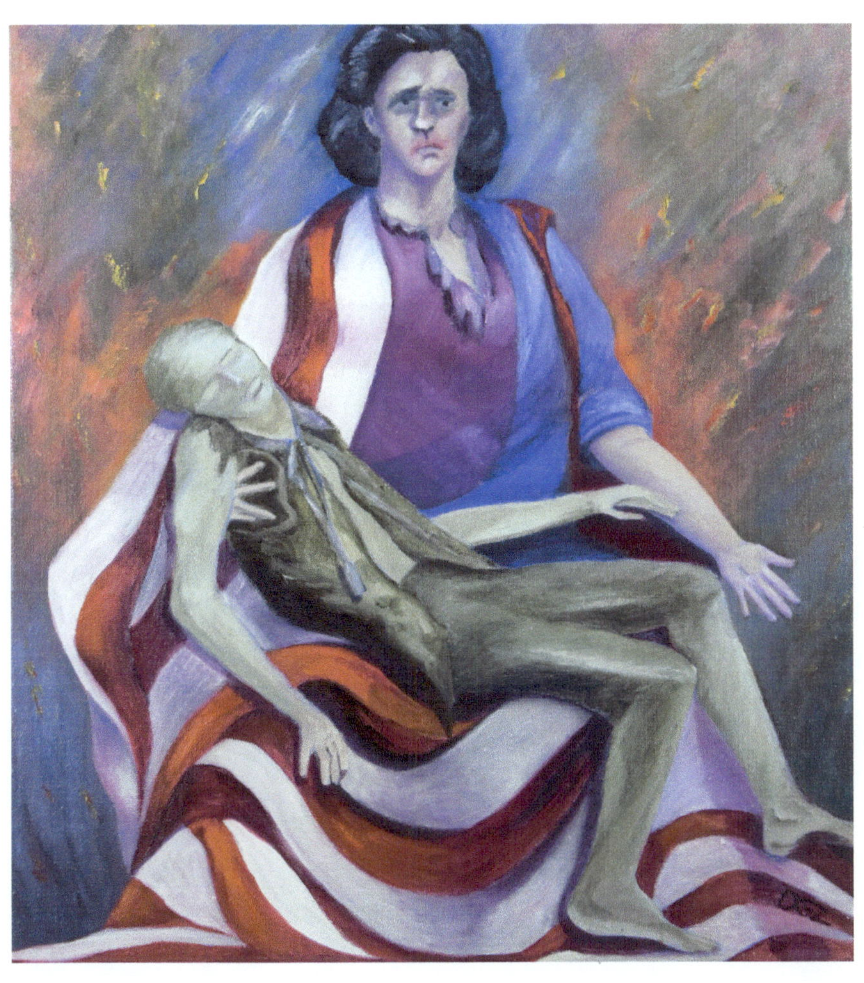

Protect Me

Protect me, if you can
From the fire and the smoke
From the poisoned waters
From the falling forests
From all the perils
Caused by my fellow man.

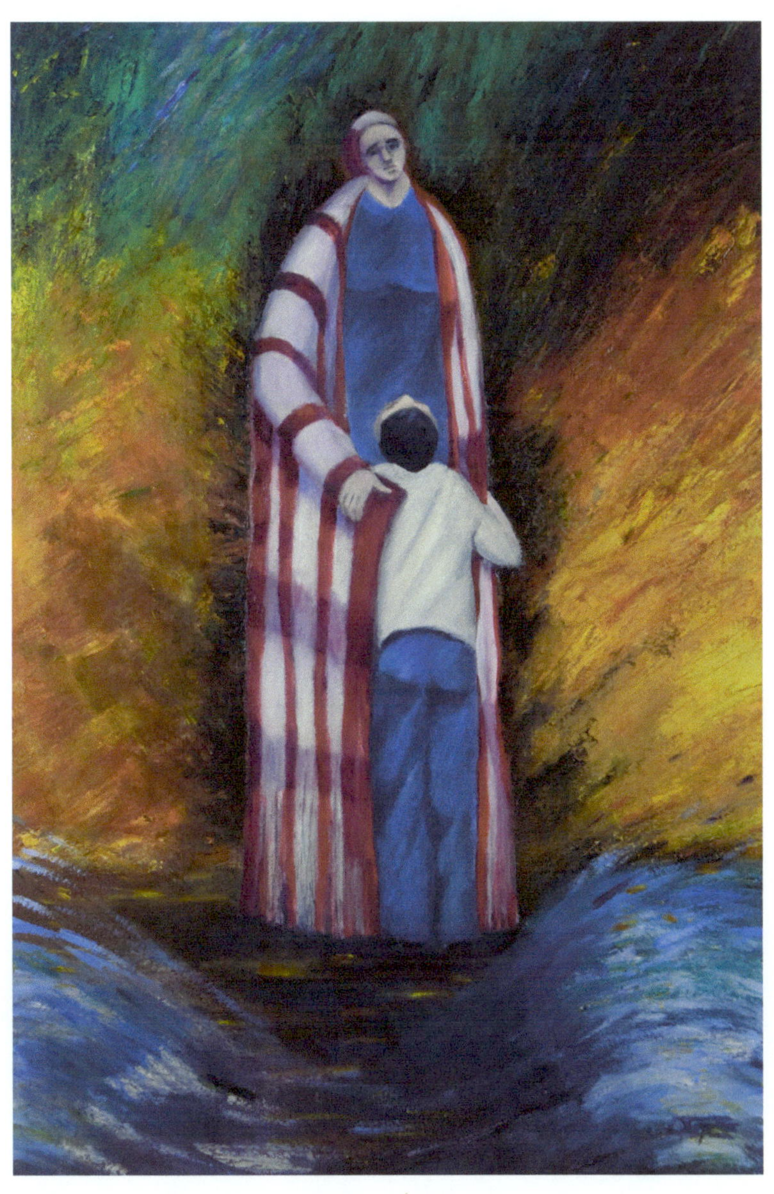

I'm Sorry, Baby

I'm sorry, baby
That I could not show you better things.
Humankind has turned to wrong,
Ugliness escaped
And took away our breath.

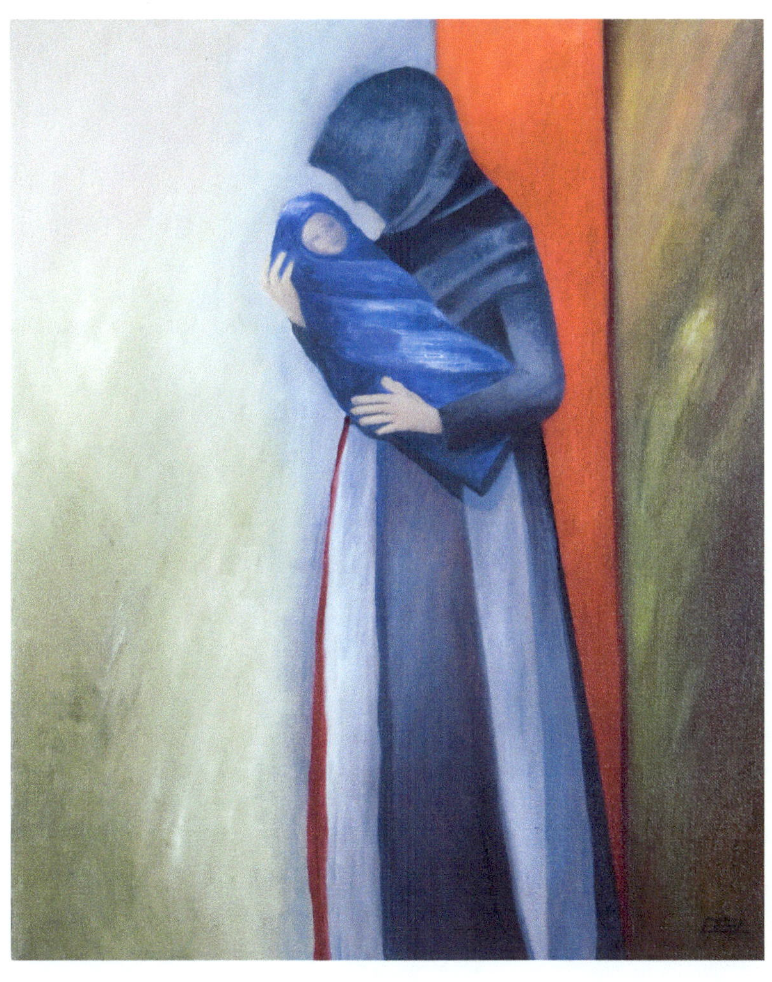

Come Home

Can you come home, my son
After what you've seen
After what you've done and what was done to you?
Can you sit at our dinner table
And tell us of your plans, your dreams?
Can you smile again with your bright eyes,
Your rosy cheeks, your laughter
That fills our hearts?
We are waiting for you.

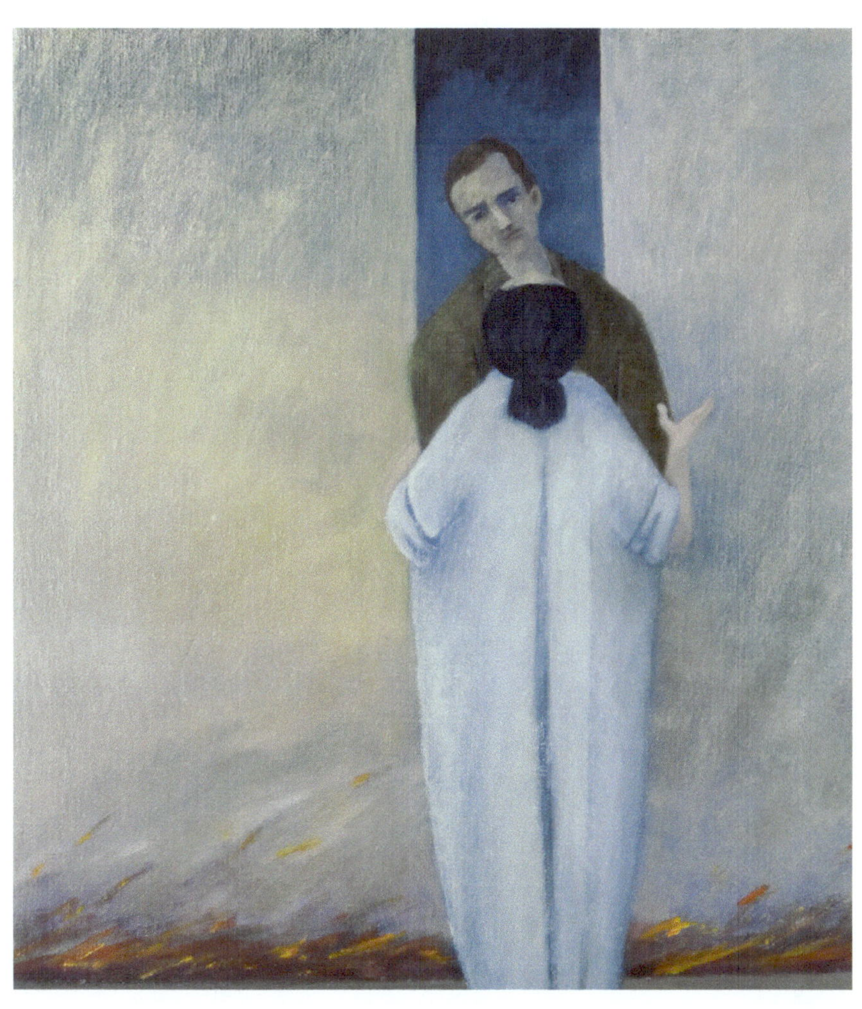

Is It Still?

Is it still so beautiful for spacious skies
When poisoned smoke is in the air
And amber waves of grain are strewn along the fields
And our majestic mountains look down at us in horror
Above the no longer fruited plain?
America, America – you've come undone
We cannot praise the good
When brotherhood is torn apart from sea to bloody sea.

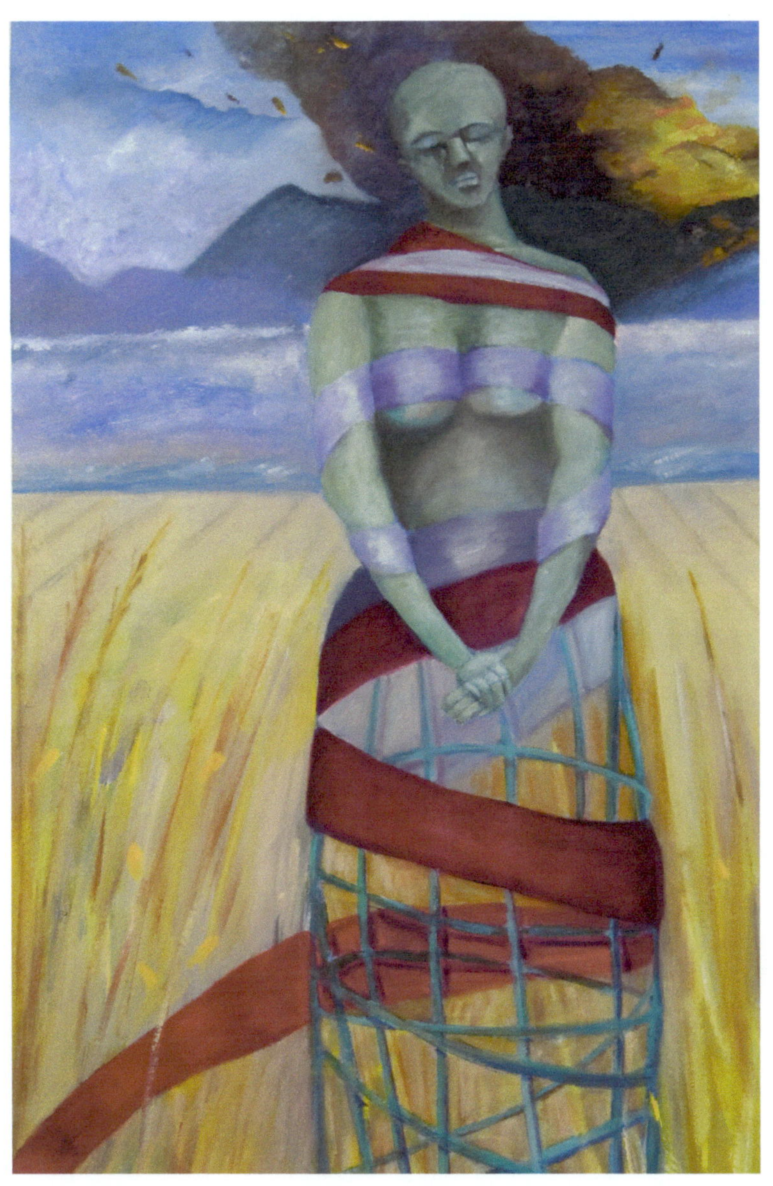

Out My Window

Out my window the smoke is rising
The land laid bare is waiting to be planted;
To produce again and give life once more
Our reason for being.

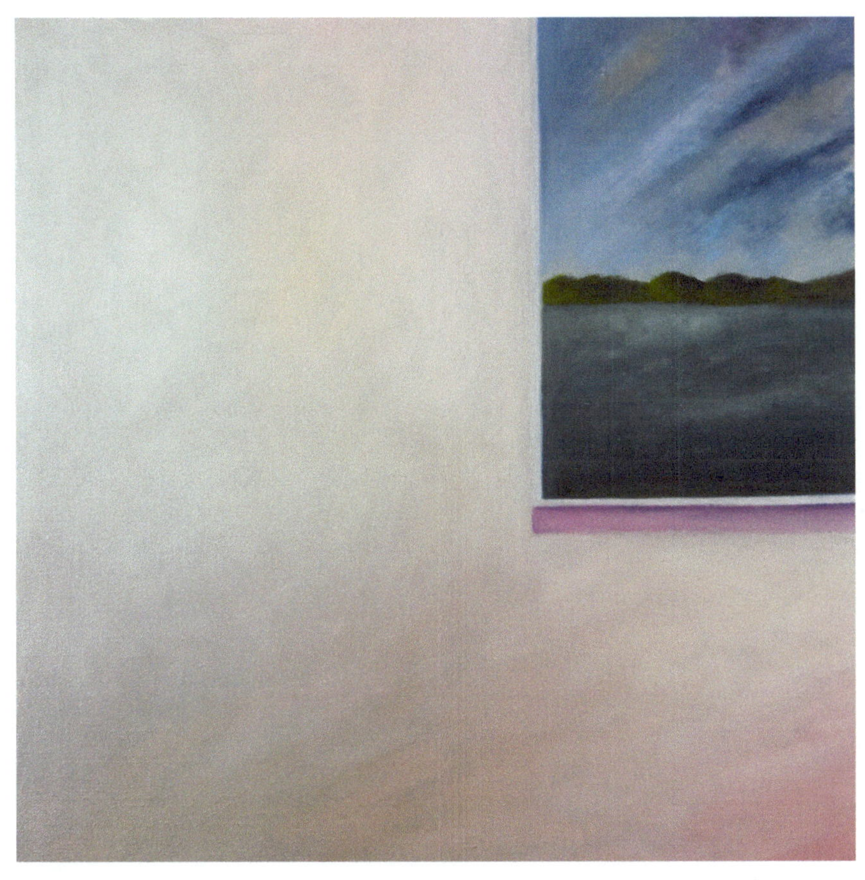

Seeds

The darkness is fading and
The sky is turning blue.
It's a nice day, mama!
Let's plant those seeds today
Can we, mama, can we?

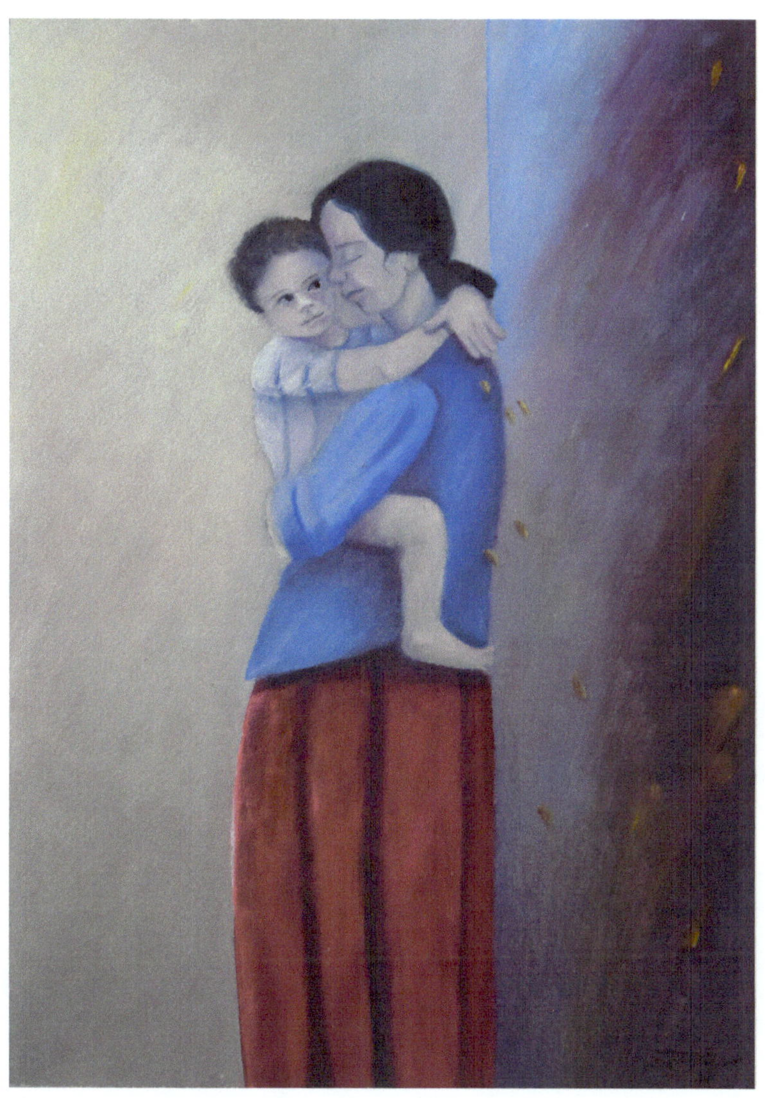

Spring

I want to think of spring
For spring brings hope.
It makes me wonder how
Life can come about again after a season of horror.
Spring turns harshness into soft
Destruction into growth
Dark to light
Gray to color.
So much is not in our control
But what do we do with what is?

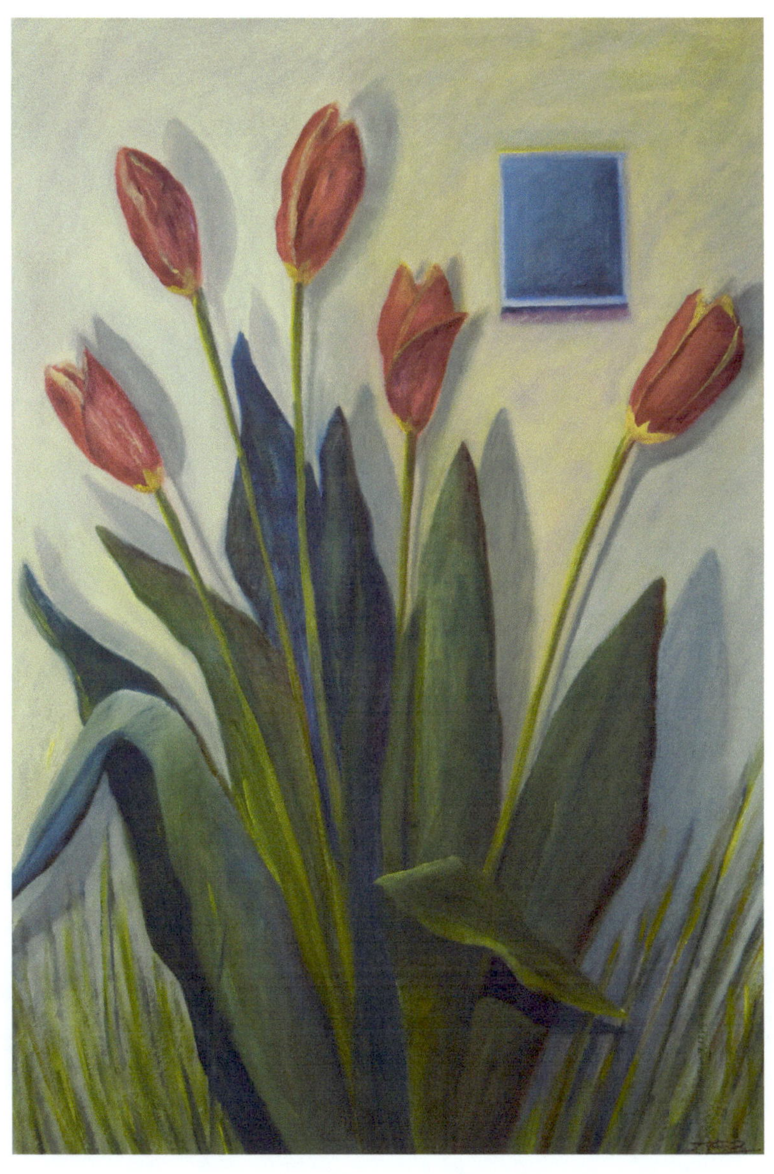

Color Plates

11. **Still Life With Tulips** (031), oil/linen, 18″x16″
13. **War** (033), oil/linen, 24″x20″
15. **Opened Window** (034), oil/linen, 18″x16″
17. **The Unempowered** (035), oil/linen, 20″x24″
19. **Fire** (036), oil/linen,11″x12″
21. **Unraveling** (037), oil/linen, 16″x24″
23. **Shrouded Figure** (038), oil/linen, 24″x16″
25. **American Gothic Shaken** (0310), oil/linen, 20″xl6″
27. **Gated Community** (0311), oil/linen, 16″x24″
29. **Peace March** (0312), oil/linen, 24″x20″
31. **Fire On The Horizon** (0313), oil/linen, 20″x24″
33. **Desolation** (0315), oil/linen, 20″x20″
35. **My Pieta** (0316), oil/linen, 20″x18″
37. **Protect Me** (0317), oil/paper, 22″x15″
39. **I'm Sorry, Baby** (0318), oil/linen, 20″x16″
41. **Come Home** (0319), oil/linen, 18″x16″
43. **Is It Still?** (0320), oil/paper, 22″x15″
45. **Out My Window** (0323), oil/linen, 20″x20″
47. **Seeds** (0321), oil/paper, 15″x11″
49. **Spring** (0322), oil/paper, 22″x15″

www.ingramcontent.com/pod-product-compliance
Lightning Source LLC
LaVergne TN
LVHW052259100826
845147LV00001B/87

* 9 7 8 0 9 8 2 3 4 8 0 7 9 *